THE NICHE
MARKETING
AND BOOK GUIDE

JENNIFER LANCASTER

Power of Words

'the riches
are in the niches'

The Niche Marketing and Book Guide.

A companion for the *Book Creation Success* club at www.BusinessAuthorAcademy.com

ISBN 978-0-9945105-2-5. A cataloguing record is available at the National Library of Australia.

(c) 2019 Jennifer Lancaster. Published by Power of Words, Australia.

Contents

What are Solo Service Providers Doing Wrong?

Rather than investing in a personal brand and offering key insights in various media, many persist in 'going wide'. So they spend on online advertising, print ads, website SEO, directory listings, radio ads: all avenues that *don't* build credibility and trust. They may get a website that has the basic pages, but it doesn't offer glimpses into who they are and what kind of 'insider' information they can help specific people with... not just 'company news', but morsels of topic expertise that you can't find anywhere else.

These excellent providers may identify as a counsellor, a therapist, a wellness coach, a financial planner, however, they don't make their point of difference and their niche target market apparent to the public. Their verbal pitch is the usual "I'm an aromatherapist", leaving you no idea of what problem they solve.

Typically, these service providers have not employed any magnetism. Being a visible spokesperson draws the right people to you (they might become followers first), rather than pushing out. Yet it's something that can be learned and achieved, just like any skill.

So How do we Tap our Magnetic Persona?

You can empower yourself with personal magnetism by building confidence with public speaking and/or with online presenting. Practical types who speak in public would benefit from working on connecting authentically, through humble openness, and rely less on PowerPoint! If you go to events a lot, perhaps note what the speaker does that connects with the audience. The Speakers Institute has many great speakers.

Whether speeches are your thing, or the written word, you can employ marketing magnetism and sales systems—even if sales is anathema to you. If you don't, basically your service is doomed to be an up-down rollercoaster of people sporadically hearing about you and timidly contacting you. And we want your business to be blooming, and blooming consistently!

If you do rely on word-of-mouth and referrals already, then a sales system with your niche target in mind is going to put that into hyperdrive. All the while, new followers and alliance partners tend to seek you out after looking at your material... just the cover of your book is sometimes enough to intrigue!

Don't be afraid to give out original information—as that's the key to your future connections.

What is Niche Marketing?

Niche Marketing aims to target a specific audience with a certain marketing and positioning strategy, rather than multiple audiences at once. This allows the business to potentially make more income —with less advertising cost.

For example, using niche marketing, a promoter for nutritional supplements would be better to target an audience of gym fanatics (with messages, brand promises, and endorsements), than to try and advertise to a mass audience with different tastes and interests. The same principle applies in book publishing. As authors, we can also use niche marketing to sell our books and content.

"TO SURVIVE IN BUSINESS, YOU'VE GOT TO APPEAR DIFFERENT"

Before I decided on my services and niche, I did a lot of research. I reviewed what other small author services/self-publishers were doing, as well as the big boys. I looked at honest reviews of author services companies and I found out the gaps in service delivery. From LinkedIn book writer groups, I found out why authors are willing to pay for certain services. A business strategist helped me with ideas about targeting my marketing towards certain business types. So my niche is book development mentoring and editing for non-fiction, and my defined target is female professionals and coaches who are time poor. Now I can find out what they really need.

When considering your niche, place yourself in the spot of leader. What will make you the leader in this area? Is it a personal experience? Is it that you've worked out the answer to problems many people have presented with?

If you are a service provider in a crowded industry (e.g. massage therapist) and you feel a micro-niche is not right for you, then consider becoming a leader for other providers in the field. Start an industry association, a regular podcast, a membership club, or put your learnings into a book or course. If you do one or two of these things well, it makes you an industry leader in that niche BY DEFAULT if no-one else is teaching/supporting these people in your country. Making more out of a business is a really motivating problem, so when you offer good support at the right prices, you'll attract followers with ease.

As a niche leader, you will be promoting a set of benefits and value that is best served by you, as the mainstream providers fight it out to serve broader markets. E.g. Designer Doorware don't just make door handles, they serve the architectural community with custom designed, quality doorware, access control and alarm systems. In many markets, we want the best provider who meets our needs exactly, not just the lowest price.

Not only is it more cost effective to practice niche marketing, but it takes a lot less time as well. With this type of marketing strategy, it is easier to reach an audience that is likely to be interested in your particular product or service. This saves money for the company, because they are able to reach an audience that is more inclined to buy than the general population, getting better results for less money.

When you think about it, Google Search is a definer of niche and micro-niche market leaders. The bots search the index for the most reputable, prolific websites whose words best represent that search phrase. The more specific the phrase, the tighter the micro-niche, and (for the business), the easier it is to be found. Google Search also takes into account social media traffic and media mentions as an indicator that a business or person is popular and relevant.

Defining a niche for yourself/your business is a process. First, you must know the problems and desires of the defined market. (Have you talked to these people over the years and asked their problems?) Second, you must determine that your business can deliver on its promises, i.e. you have strong experience in the core aspects of the business.

Growing the niche takes a further two steps. First, you must ensure the basic message is coming across. You need everyone you meet to understand what's unique about what you do. This might be called a 'pitch', but I prefer your '**magnetic calling card**'. Get this right and your prospect will soon make him or herself known to you.

On a larger scale, your niche marketing collateral has to be crystal clear, consistent, and targeted to the reader/prospect.

The second part is growing your expert leader status. As a leader, you need to have a solid reputation and credibility. This can be built up by being a voice in the industry, such as writing in trade magazines and leading blogs, writing website content, offering free reports or guides to new leads, belonging to the industry association, speaking at events, gathering a social media following, and by writing a book on the subject. All content written to attract a market is called 'content marketing'.

> "The ideal position is to craft your own niche where no one else makes their living in the same way, in the same place, at the same time. There are no competitors. You are unique. You have a place in the economy of nature."
> — Richard Koch, author 'The Star Principle' and 'The 80/20 Principle'.

Why Do Authors Put Off Their Marketing?

At author meets and on email, I seem to have struck a similarity between when authors think it would be time to build their author platform and promote their book.

"I will focus on that when I've finished my final draft"
"I will start planning the marketing when I've got my production (cover, edits) done"
"I am in creative mode now, so I will worry about that when I am uploading and launching".

Basically, they are putting off till tomorrow what they could (and probably should) be doing NOW. Admittedly, it might help to have named your book title and come up with the angle. But you don't need to wait any longer than that... plus, fame as an author never happens overnight. It is a long, slow road, best taken one pitch, tweet, or post at a time. More on this in "Selling your Books".
But before you go ahead with promotion plans, first do some work on your ideal reader — or Tribe.

Who makes up my Tribe?

Males/Females who love _____

who are aged _____ parent or child-free _____

whose support needs are _____

in business or employed? _____

time poor or money poor? _____

So, once you've determined your tribe and you know your broad topic area, then you need to find what they MOST want to know and how they like to learn. You can do this by:

- A Survey (online or at events)
- Poll inside a LinkedIn group or Meetup group
- Use Amazon as a search engine to find the popular topics in your category.

Determining your Tribe's Needs

You can't please everyone with one offering, so don't try. Consider your tribe's probable gender, age group, interests, and common pain points. But don't just guess; you'll have to investigate to really understand their frustrations. Ideally ask a client what is missing from the present service, what they would like to achieve more of, and get her to talk you through her vision of what is really needed in this area. Don't fret if you're yet to attract a client. When we're starting out we don't have clientele, but we still have our own troubles and our research.

Are you the *before* and the *after* of your target market? Then there is a vulnerability that you need to share. Open up and tell the story of how terrible it was before you discovered this method (or the missing link). Or if not you, tell case studies of clients, including the problems before, and the results and benefits of the new system or service you created.

The great thing about knowing your tribe is you can create a series of books, a course, or audios/digital download products to appeal to them. What's easiest for you—and easiest for them to access?

Once you know the exact WHO, along with your own WHY, your whole branding and book cover images can be designed to appeal to your tribe and their needs. Sometimes their need is for inner peace, and this conjures up calming colours and flowing design elements. Sometimes their need is for empowerment, and this conjures up strong colours and symbols that represent growth (trees, flowers).

Jennifer Lancaster

First Steps to Creating your Book

Finding the Message in a Book

Every single-message book has a hidden question. Why do some nationalities eat lovely food but never gain weight?... "French Women Don't Get Fat".

"How can I manage my own finances myself and not get ripped off?"... was the hidden question behind my book "How to Control your Financial Destiny".

What are the three questions that crop up on your deathbed?... "Life's Golden Ticket".

You have a really important message to share, and it could be from something clients keep telling you, or something you realised after many years of banging your head. You don't necessarily have to relate your story in a memoir, because it could be better to recount just one experience and develop deeper material based on that learning. (Anyway, many of us find everyday people's memoirs unbearable, because it doesn't relate back to us).

Bernadette Jiwa (author of *Make Your Idea Matter* and *Difference* and winner of Australia's Best Business Blog 2012) confesses that she picked some of the most popular topics from her blog to include in her earlier books. Her book's single message is often the thing that up-and-coming entrepreneurs want to know.

Timing is crucial with putting forth a strong message; too late and you'll be among the many, too early and you'll need a huge momentum. Above all, you must be a leader and show that you have fresh ideas.

Create Articles First

To get your thoughts crystal clear, what about creating a series of articles? Then find an ideal target audience magazine that is possibly interested in publishing them. Consider good digital magazines as well. Approach local editors first if you're starting out; the smaller publications are more open to new talent. If you're not an excellent article writer, you might need some editing help!

Aim to build a co-operative arrangement with the publication that is read by your market. You might need to place an advertisement to get your foot in the door, as they favour advertisers, or join a network. Magazines open to co-operative editorials or articles:

www.mattersmagazine.com.au (Mini write-up, editorials, Sunshine Coast, print / digital)
https://smallville.com.au/become-a-contributor/ (long-term contributors only)
www.coachinglife.com.au (Print & digital. Pitch or submit a long article about coaching)
www.womensnetwork.com.au/promotion/publications/ (It helps to be a member)

You will notice that these magazines offer either low-cost advertising options or free submissions if you're an excellent writer with a fresh topic. I'm not suggesting mainstream magazines for most authors for the reasons that very few advertisers get good ROI (return on investment) and the audience is too broad.

Defamation, Copyright & Libel

1)   If what you say is true, it cannot be libel.
2)   If the person written about is dead, you can't libel them[1]

'Defamatory' statements harm the reputation of the person who's the subject of the statement. Libel law means writers must be certain that what they write is true; so check all the facts you have 'read online'. If you can't verify a fact as true or false, then it's an opinion. Try not to portray opinions as facts.

Copyright Act 1968 states that it is unlawful to rework someone else's text and call it your own. You can read it if you like, but this legislation is 591 pages long.

You'll probably be using some quotes or paraphrases from other authors, so mind your copyright laws. Australian Copyright Council can help with author queries and free legal advice on copyright periods, how to find the copyright owner, etc. Copyright Clearance Center (US) is a service where you can ask for permission to use certain quotes and phrases from a book published through traditional publishers internationally.

---

1   source: "Keep it Real: creative non-fiction", Lee Gutkind.

It is advised to put (c) Your Name, Year on the first page of a manuscript. "All rights reserved" means that you are not allowing any infringement of the usual copyright laws, any copying of content, etc. Also put the country in which it is published.

Moral rights are personal rights, which *"Protect their reputation by protecting the integrity of the work they've produced".* [2]

Copyright laws do not apply to book titles or pen-names, and you cannot claim ownership on them. If you have a unique system/brand name, you could choose to lodge a Trademark for that name. See **https://www.ipaustralia.gov.au**

Another great idea for business book writers and others is to create visual model. Visual models are your unique spin on a technique, an acronym explanation, or system of six steps. Although you are the one to come up with the acronym descriptions or outline of the system, a skilled graphic designer can create a simple visual representation to help readers 'get it'.

Using a visual model in your promotional arsenal can also help lift your book above the masses.

--> To inspire yourself, see: **https://bookauthority.org/books/best-storytelling-books**

Creating a Winning Title

Be clear to potential readers. Find a title that enhances your brand and tells people about the theme you cover in the book.

> "The purpose of a title is to grab the reader's attention and make him want to get his hands on the book" (Robert Bly)

Think about the human drives when naming your book and creating content. Does the book offer the reader:

- Social belonging or love
- Control / security
- Achievement / growth
- Recognition / need to contribute?

---

2   source: "The Writer's Guide", Irina Dunn.

The very popular Dale Carnegie book "How to Win Friends and Influence People" was a title that carries an emotional driver—the need to belong and make friends. 'How to' titles are very easy to engage people who are wanting to learn something. (I used them a lot!)

A benefit that appeals to your market contained in the title is ideal for an unknown author. e.g. "The No-Lose Guide to Hiring Sub-Contractors".

More title tips:
- A short title combined with a long sub-title (explaining the benefit or the type of reader) often works well.
- It must concisely state what the book will deliver, and not throw the reader off-kilter.
- Try to include the terms that your reader will enter in a search window when looking for a book.
- Try to make the main title brief enough to show up clearly in a thumbnail (small image).
- You can be a little quirky in the title or the subtitle, but perhaps not both.

A Word on Keywords

If you use good keywords in your book title (or short eBook title), this will help your book get found when people search in Google or Amazon. In addition, build these words into your blog's posts. Variations of keyword phrases can work, like for example:

Simple Ways to *Find Friends*
How to Build Friendships that Last
Female Friendships: How to Make them Smoother

Amazon and the Print on Demand suppliers use keywords to help readers find titles in a niche topic. Your book will rarely appear alone among these search results.

For Amazon, you are advised *not* to put any of your title or subtitle words into the keywords section. You need to use keywords to capture themes in your book which are applicable to the content and searched for by normal users every day, e.g. a book on home loans could have "mortgages" or "line of credit" as a keyword, but not "bad debt".

Blog Content

As more and more of us look for solutions to our problems online, it's fruitful to use solution-based headings to capture our target readers. An author blog or themed website is the best place to build this content. Some authors offer a free chapter and a free worksheet to encourage new readers. Then they can market to their email list.

An Author Banner is one way to transform a plain vanilla web theme and make it beautiful, personal and professional. These cost around $50 - $120, depending whether ordering online or via a graphic designer, like Ngirl Design.

Common Trim Types/Book Sizes

Inches	mm	Binding type	Paper stock	Application ideas
5.5 x 8.5	216 x 140	Perfect, hardcover, cloth	creme/white	BW/color
5.83 x 8.27	210 x 148 (A5)	Perfect	creme/white	100-200 pages text
6 x 9	229 x 152	Perfect, hardcover, cloth	creme/white	140-250 pages text
8.5 x 8.5	216 x 216 (square)	Perfect, hardcover	white	Portfolio / design
8.26 x 11.69	297 x 210 (A4)	Perfect (or stapled)	white	Manual, min 64 pp.
8 x 10	276 x 203	Perfect	white	Photo book

IngramSpark provides more than 23 book sizes and allows for saddle stitch, perfect bound, and some hardcover types. Most authors choose perfect bound on black and white. Most of the books ship from Melbourne, however, bulk copies freighted can cost a fair bit.

Colour printing also has three choices, from standard, standard 70 (105gsm), to premium, with its better definition and paper thickness. Print prices rise steeply with colour options. With print on demand, you cannot select just some pages to be colour plates. You cannot switch from colour to black and white after online set-up either. It is best to order at least 1 print proof and then 40-100 author books. If you're a first time author, do not order hundreds of books without 100 pre-orders all lined up.

You can choose from Gloss or Matt covers. If deliberating over colour print, order a sample book set from IngramSpark. Note that you cannot choose embossed, gold, or UV spot with these printing types. Have a play with the Ship & Print Calculator to determine book costs:
https://www.ingramspark.com/resources/tools

Then ensure that quantities of this size will have produce enough royalty to make a profit after production, using their Publisher Compensation calculator.

Why a Print Book?

Unless writing for fulfillment, think of paperback books first as a marketing tool, and then as a revenue generator. Most books self-published without a flurry of activity will struggle to return their own costs. To really engage your ideal market is (almost) priceless, and it's going to ensure your profits in your main business.

With good timing, correct alignment to your purpose, and serendipitous help from a publishing coach and editor, your book can become the vehicle for opportunity, growth and new leads.

How Long Before Launch Should Book Files be Ready?

In the normal bookshop distribution world, we'd say 3-6 months. But when you're self-publishing without bookstore distribution, your files should be converted to ePubs and your print file should be print ready about 6-7 weeks prior to a publicised book launch. This is for a new publisher, and 4 weeks for an old hand.

This is because your cover and interior file has to be approved by the platform (e.g. IngramSpark or Lulu) and released, then approved again at the online retailer (e.g. Barnes & Noble). You'll also need to proof any print book, which is sent via post or courier. You might want to allow another 10 days in case there is a fixable fault with the print proof.

Pre-Publication Activities

In this time, if your focus is on Amazon for example, you will need to step through an online tax interview. After ensuring the right author name, you fill out your TFN or ABN under Tax ID at Amazon Kindle Direct (**KDP.com**). Unless of course you don't mind the IRS taking 30% withholding tax of non-US residents income. As an Australian resident without a US business, you can claim the tax treaty with Australia, at 5% tax on sales in US. IngramSpark allows this by using the author's business status and ABN (Australian Business Number). Lulu allows it by filling out a tax form and sending it via email.

This is a good time to read success stories on Amazon launches. Sometimes a launch strategy means eBook giveaways, e.g. 1 week free, then revert to $4.99 (see Amazon Select), but not always. You can give away your book directly as well, right from a link on the Amazon book page. Goodreads also allow book giveaways in particular countries.

Too busy? Hire a Virtual Assistant to request endorsements and reviews for your pre-publication book (called Pre-Reading Copies or PRC). Send your own personal connections (in a related business) a copy, along with a request for endorsement.

What about Selling the Books or eBooks?

Here is a simple break-down of the steps towards a non-fiction book launch.

Brand:
Set up your author brand colours (two is good), theme (e.g. saving money is mine), and get some initial author photos done. You'll need another photo with the book cover later, which will contain your chosen colours. Working with a graphic designer will help to ensure your brand is awesome, from the typeface chosen down to the relevant logo for your imprint.

Pitch:
You need to get your media pitch ready. Firstly, what timely/newsworthy angle might you create, and secondly, summarise what your book is about.

Example Angle: Isn't it crazy how Australians get scammed more than $21 million a year, when they really aimed to invest for wealth?

Example Pitch: My new book, Creative with Money, helps people understand how past scammers or spruikers have operated and ties it in with examples of how our emotions get in the way of investing success. (There is much more that I didn't add in here).

Produce:
Your book must represent the highest quality that you can muster. It's representing your talent and so must be edited and formatted properly. Beautifully simple covers create a desire to click on to read more, while busy, ugly ones detract and even repel.

Promote:

Promotion isn't just plugging your book on launch. It's doing a host of activities that are connected with you as a writer (rather than just personal). So set up your 3-4 social media profiles to say 'author', some with your book cover, and reflect this theme and brand.

The articles (or journal papers or essays) you write to promote your discoveries, your theories, and your research will all help to create a desire for a longer piece – your upcoming book. Some magazines will pay for quality submissions of a certain length. We go into creating magazine articles just for book promotion in the next chapter.

Then on launch, you can start sharing an excerpt of the book with relevant magazines, journals and so on. Looking for wide circulation, don't be fussy whether the publication is online or offline. You can check article-share numbers by searching on 'BuzzSumo' for your topic specifically.

It's also wise to track your pitches to the news media within a CRM system, one that allows reminders to follow-up. You can follow up an emailed pitch by phone (if you have their number) or send out a sample or colour advance media sheet to the editors. Persistence will pay!

If every media pitch fails, you can always post articles direct to your LinkedIn and share with your network. But don't give up at the first 'no response'; it pays to ask more questions and get in touch in a new way (tweet / message / phone call). Journalists' and editors' email inboxes are overflowing with stuff and so a new pitch often gets missed.

If you plan to speak at seminars, networking events, or exhibit at expos, then you'll have a forum to sell many print books. If you don't have the capacity to do this, then why not set up Strategic Alliance partners to help sell your book while you're working. Choose known speakers and trainers who have a synergy with your stance on your subject.

To sell eBooks through others, it's fairly inexpensive to set up for affiliates with ShareaSale, ClixGalore, or similar, but you'll need to have some leeway in pricing for their share of the profits. You'll also need some professional website banners made up, a sales 'hook', and 3D book covers to make the books sell much better. These are all very easy to buy from the top-rated sellers at **Fiverr.com**.

Selling Books via Your Website

When you've already expended $3,000-5,000 to edit and produce your book, the realisation that you need a website to promote it online might elicit these two questions:

1. Do I create a book website or an author website?
2. How do I get a good result without busting my bank account?

There are a few more things to consider as well, so let's open this can of worms now. You'll need to know how to upload new book details, social share posts, and post articles and media mentions. You'll need to realise that in websites, *free* isn't without cost, and the choice of a supported pro theme is a good idea. (A free theme could leave you with a non-working website down the track).

Another aspect is, rolling with the times, your brand will grow and change. If you set up a 'book' domain and website, unless you have some expert support, you may not have enough time to justify a one-book-one-website approach. But... with your Author Website, just like JennieBrown.com.au or JenniferLancaster.com.au (or a niche name), the site can be added to and morph over a decade or so, as you put out more products for your growing number of fans. Better still, you can capture reader or fan emails with an offer, like the first chapter of your book.

Below, I have two options depending on your ambitions online.

Author Website Design Recommendations

Option 1: Novice to websites and low budget

For novices to website design, I recommend the bare minimum of:

1. Buying your 'name' or 'business name' domain name.

2. Use Square (Weebly), the all-in-one platform. It may not rank as well, but it's simple to set up and costs from $US88 per year to take off their logos and add some functions, like a store. It takes the hassles out of hosting and constant plugin updating.

Squarespace is another simple option, which costs around $16-22 per month (they host) and uses design templates. It is supported and has video tutorials.

Option 2: Future proof your Web presence

If however you want to continually add and share articles, host a branded website, and possibly add a store, then Wordpress hosted on your domain name is the best bet. Many website hosts let customers install Wordpress through an easy order form. Others offer installation for a small fee.

Next, order some vibrant web banners containing your author photo and book cover, of the right size for your desired header image (usually extra wide). Designers can blend several elements together while sticking to your brand colours. Try PeoplePerHour or Fiverr.

WPBakery is a page builder app that gives multiple ways to control the design, colours, and icons of every page. Designers and novices alike can use it after some tutorials available from WPBakery.

Of course, with the many plugins and widgets, a novice will take time to learn how a WordPress website setup actually works. (It's taken me several years and I still call on technical help for things like plugin breakdowns, from time to time). If this all sounds like too many hours work to you, then order Website Design from a professional designer. Ensure that the person has designed websites for authors before, because your needs are different. Web Hosting is an additional charge.

WordPress Plugins for Authors

Do you want your own online bookstore at nil cost? Then access these little gems through the "plugins" section of a Wordpress-based site. Plugins are not for WordPress.com, but WordPress, the open source CMS.

MyBookTable. A WordPress Plugin to help authors sell more books and make affiliate money through sites like Amazon and Barnes & Noble. It features social media sharing and you can also link their app on your Facebook author page. To get book affiliate commissions you must upgrade to an API key, which is $49 for 1 domain.

Mooberry Books. It is a plugin very similar to Mybooktable, just with a different look and feel. In the options you can also add your local bookstores, like Fishpond.

> JetPack for WordPress (**https://jetpack.com**) is an optional extra that saves time in administering your website, if you do not have a website administrator. It helps with publishing tools, back up, plug-in updates, security, speed, and SEO plugin.
>
> It costs around US$39 p.a. for hobbyists.

They both work similarly; you just copy and paste your book information and buy links. You can allow people to buy directly from you by putting in a special Paypal button link as a custom retail option. You probably won't need a Woocommerce shopping cart (a plugin), unless you are selling many other items.

Design Styles

What you must remember is… BIG.

You want your book to stand out big and bold on the page, with solid endorsements or reviews as a graphic underneath. Beside the book cover (hopefully in 3D), put a couple of hot selling points. Don't forget any 'media mentions'; it all helps. If desired, offer a 10-page preview as a download.

If your book has reviews on Goodreads, then MyBookTable can feed those reviews into your page once the Goodreads link is placed.

WordPress Themes for Authors

Like a complex design skin, the theme lets you customise to your desired menu, navigation styles, sidebars, header images, normal page as a home page, blog widgets, etc. Theme shopping starts out quite fun... but about 8 hours and 40 theme options later, your head is spinning! So let me recommend some options based on experience.

1) *Impreza.* JenniferLancaster.com.au is based on this adaptable theme, and it's customisable with a builder app like WPBakery, or just use the WP Block editor. Buy on ThemeForest. You will need some idea of how to customise a theme if doing it yourself, but if you get stuck, there are WordPress pros on the WordPress forums to help out.

2) *Bridge.* Creative best-selling blog theme (magazine look), WordPress. Includes updates. US$59. See **https://1.envato.market/KEnEv**

Buying a theme is not the end of the story, as it then has to be customised for your brand. There is about ten+ hours of work to make it look right, plus hosting setup, so perhaps employ a website design professional to do this. Envato offer a theme set-up service to install it, but this is not the same as customisation. Customising means fixing brand colours, creating particular images of yours, creating better-looking titles, setting up the blog page, laying out the home page, installing a contact form and opt-in offer, and putting in the correct widgets.

A Myriad of Ways to Sell Books, Courses, eBooks

Webinars also lend themselves to selling ebooks. You can even offer to talk on a compatible expert's webinar and make a special offer at the end. (Set this offer up at different remote locations prior to the audience joining the webinar). However, pro-level webinar launch software (e.g. WebinarJam) costs plenty (US$69 pm), so you can start off with Zoom Webinars at a low start cost of AU$21 pm (one host). See **https://zoom.us/pricing**.

Videos that are 'how to' or 'inside secrets' style are also very good for attracting your ideal customer to your products. Brendon Burchard is the master at producing simple videos, offered with a simple landing page. There's not many sales calls to action but it is there when you're ready. Use a clean and simple video frame, such as Vimeo or Jetpack Business.

Landing pages rule. 'Sack Your Financial Planner' sold with a one-page sales letter online attached to online advertising. I didn't offer incentives, but I had my photo with the book and spoke to their feelings about financial planners. The sales conversion rate was 10% from paid clicks—later I learned that this was damn good! See **Convertkit.com** for a landing page and email marketing tool (tech-savvy users).

Facebook is ideal for sharing interesting graphics, leading to more likes, more shares, and more book interest. Engage an audience with square pics with quotable quotes, an infographic made for you, a cartoon made for you, or something else. See **fiverr.com** and **peopleperhour.com** for ideas of what clever people can create for you.

Helping browsers become readers via Facebook should be easy—but it's not. There is an **author app** to let folks preview 10 pages of your book and have a link to buy it. If you published on Amazon, inside Facebook go to "Author Marketing App". It's free to install, but rarely does much for sales.

While there is a 'ViewInside widget' that costs, you can utilise Smashwords and Kindle's book widgets for free if you're clever. Use these graphical book widgets on your website to let readers view some of the book easily. Ironically, they work best in the sidebar widget (HTML code): a widget inside a widget. Smashwords book widgets look terrific and can include the price. Amazon widgets all look different, depending on which elements and final size you select.

Zoho Social is a free or paid platform, where you can schedule social updates in one go. You can make various graphic or text posts about your book's content. More advanced scheduling is available on upgrade. I use ZohoSocial's extension (on Chrome) because it saves time by allowing quick-shares and following activity for Facebook, LinkedIn, Twitter, and Facebook Page; you can also share your blog post image to Instagram through their mobile app.

Use **BookLink (http://booklinker.net/)** to make an appropriate link to sell to Amazon stores from the one URL... So when marketing globally, the buyer is taken straight to their own country's Amazon bookstore. It tracks all visitors.

Advertising, Schmadvertising

You might have heard of promoting your book through Facebook ads, boosts, and also via sites like BookBub – paying to sell it. However, there is some evidence that this may not help non-business authors. According to a survey of 105 authors by *Writing for a Living*, mainly novelists, 60% thought that paid Facebook Marketing wasn't worth it, with another 20% not sure (which means, probably not). The exception would be if you are using your book as a "loss leader", because you anticipate that readers will later become interested prospects or students.

Another thing that definitely does not work is spruiking your book promos in author and book Facebook groups. (If you run your own group or the group is all made up of friends, that is not the same case). Instead, focus on how book publicity is done professionally.

Traditional book publicists for business authors target these types of media:
- Print – magazines and newspapers
- Broadcast – TV and radio (and don't forget being a guest on hot Podcasts)
- Online outlets – e.g. Entrepreneur (for US); Roooar magazine, Dynamic Business, Inside Small Business (for Aust), Women's Network magazine (book review).
- The author's local media – eg. Local free magazines, guides, newspapers and Rotary newsletters.

"Bylined articles are often important when promoting business experts. The author writes articles about a topic related to the book. It can be a "how to," "top five tips," or case study where the author showcases how his ideas and expertise solve a problem."
– Smith Publicity

The goals of gaining book publicity are to:
- showcase the author's knowledge or life experience
- go after speaking engagements, leading to personal sales
- highlight success of the author's business, and
- create the awareness that might spark book sales.

Do you see how this differs to outright advertising of a book?

A handy *Australian media guide*, including some easier-to-access magazines, will be included in month 3 of **Book Creation Success** membership at **https://www.BusinessAuthorAcademy.com**.

P.O.D. Book Distribution Partners

Using IngramSpark, there are agreements to approve your book for sale in the US, UK/Europe and Australia if you wish, at retail prices you approve first. LSI/IngramSpark have distribution to:

US
Ingram
Amazon.com
Barnes & Noble
Baker & Taylor
Espresso Book Machine

UK / Europe
Adlibris
Amazon.com
Book Depository Ltd
Books Express
Eden Interactive
Gardners
Paperback Shop

Superbookdeals
... and 11 more.

Australia / New Zealand
The Nile (online bookstore)
James Bennett*, Peter Pal (library suppliers)
ALS (library supplier)*
University Co-op Bookshop
Booktopia (online bookstore)
Rainbow Book Agencies

*Back this up with emailing them a new title listing as well. Notify library suppliers if you supply bulk orders direct, and you might just get some orders.

Writing the Content of Your Book

Once you know your target market intimately, then it's much easier to plan the outline of your book. Writers (including myself) who start writing a book without any plan tend to end up spending too much time later cutting out repeated segments and getting in a dither about the structure. So that's why this stage is important.

Outlining and Structuring Tools

You start with your 'tribe' in mind and a list of their most-wanted questions or desires. If you don't know these, then use some topics you've thought of as keywords in a Google search. Are people excitedly asking questions on forums about this? Are there searches for this topic showing up in Google Trends? If so, these are both good signs. You can also combine this broad research with more personal surveys where you ask specific questions to find out what your tribe wants.

Rather than getting too long a list, first Mind Map™ the central theme/topic on a big sheet of paper. Let your mind run free and expand the sub-topics naturally from each other, with adjoining lines. After the process of expanding out topics is finished, whittle them down to just those that should resonate with your audience and are aligned to your message.

For those research-based writers, try Scrivener's 30-day trial (**https://www.literatureandlatte.com/scrivener/overview**) for outlining and arranging your notes. It's a cloud project management and word processing software that allows users (for US$45) to "outline and structure your ideas, take notes, view research alongside your writing and compose the constituent pieces of your text in isolation or in context".

A **Developmental Editor** can also help with theming and structuring at the first stages of writing. Our *writing mentoring service* combines developmental work with mentoring to help authors feel confident in their book's direction and content, and grow as a writer.

Writing Voice

The writer's voice is important to engage the final readers to: a) keep reading, and b) fill in a good review. Have you been taught to write inside academia? The habits you picked up there may not be serving your audience now, as you don't want your voice to sound preachy, dry or too formal. It's all about creating that connection.

If you're writing a book for non-professionals, then of course you may put in some known colloquisms, use contractions, and even put in your own side confessions in order to build a connection with the reader.

Keeping the flow is equally important. There are little words you can put in to connect one sentence to the next, then one paragraph to the next. If you jump between smaller topics inside the chapter, then perhaps use a sub-heading, like I've done here.

Find the Hot Selling Points

As you expand your topics, start looking for what Judy Cullins (book coach) calls "the nine hot selling points". Nine is up to you, for me, five or six will do. For example, my eBook *How to Control Your Financial Destiny* had these hot selling points, which arouse curiousity:

- Don't just get mad with financial planners for lousy performance, get even!
- Find out why *you're* the one to create your financial plan
- *Discover* how to protect your wealth
- *Learn* why leveraging makes one wealth vehicle a better option
- *Why* paying down your home loan first may not be the right thing to do.

"Stories explain and benefits sell" - Judy Cullins.

Most readers need strong reasons to buy a book. The benefits actually give them those reasons. If you don't intimately know the benefits of reading your book, then how can you summarise it in the blurb or sales page? So jot down 5-6 specific benefits of your content.

You can also *go long* with benefits. With an online sales page, you have room to offer many more little teasers. Bob Bly (**https://www.bly.com**) is the master at selling eBooks from his own sales

---

Never Forget Book Endorsements

Another thing to do in 'pre-sales' is to gather endorsements for your book. After a request by phone or email, 'pre-print' copies are sent to author celebrities or industry leaders to review, and if your book is up to standard, then they might send a short endorsement. If you have no publicist, then you'll do this job.

The endorsements then go into the front pages or the back cover of your book, so it's important to deadline the return for these before the book cover is due for design. Give them 2-3 weeks notice at the very least.

The power of the endorsement is two-fold. An outside source stating how good they think the book is carries weight, and if that source is known and trusted by the reader to be a leader in the field, then that trust flows through to your book.

Look around; there are many contactable leaders in your field. They may have written a book themselves and are open to an exchange of endorsements, or they may just realise that this small gift of their time is important to you. Always thank them profusely and highlight a link to their own book on one of your website sales pages.

---

pages. There is a formula where he makes the reader want to find out the 'recipe' that he teases in his sales page. You won't see these pages until you sign up for his email newsletter.

Video Trailers

Some of these selling points can also be made into a **video trailer**. I got an amateur book trailer with a Fiverr seller for about $15, which I used in a presentation. Box of Crayons made a much fancier video for the release of *The Alchemy of Great Work*, which is worth checking out on YouTube.

There are many tools to make your own. Try *Lumen5* for creating videos from your blog posts. If subscribing to Creative Cloud, you get *Adobe Spark* (simple image and video-maker) for free. You can make a video or Instagram post with pre-made backgrounds, with your brand fonts. Whatever you do, don't buy a glitzy video trailer 'package' from a vanity press, because you are not going to make that money back. The key to book buzz is in your fan base and the angle, not simply the video production. See PewdePie, millionaire vlogger, if you don't believe me!

What Platforms for eBooks?

Mostly authors choose to hire a freelancer like myself to help format eBook files. But if you really want to go direct, you have to know which platform uses which format. Adobe Digital Editions use the format '.ePub', the most common form of eBook today, which can be read on desktops, tablets and e-readers.

IngramSpark allows for distribution to Apple, so you may not need to go direct. The Apple iBookstore requires that you upload an EPUB (for normal iBooks) or an iBOOKS file (for Multi-Touch books), so Ingram ask for a checked ePub file.

While **Smashwords** offers wide distribution and a range of formats, their technical formatting requirements means time fussing with document settings, unless already done. For Word-to-ebook and simple aggregation, I recommend **Draft2Digital** for indie authors. At either you will need to do the tax interview online to prove you are not a US citizen or US-based and thus claim the discounted tax treaty (5% withholding tax for Australians rather than 30%).

Google Play allows you to upload EPUB or PDF. Not many eBook distributors bother listing on Google Play because of a lack of sales. See **https://play.google.com/books/publish/u/0/**

Pubit and **Kindle Direct Publishing** (**http://kdp.com**) welcome Word documents. If you have an InDesign book, then you'll want to convert it to ePub (with Navigable contents) for directly uploading in the right format. However, this end file rarely works and passes ePub check, and so it is better to pay a freelancer to convert the book properly into .ePub and .mobi format for Kindle.

Conversion processes to make a viable ePub file are notoriously difficult—my advice is to save yourself the time and pain and get a professional to do it. Most covers require a particular size and dimension and many retailers reject an eBook with an incorrect cover size or type. (It should be a single cover JPEG at 72 dots per inch, 2:3 dimension).

The rule for ebook selling is: *The more Platforms the better!*

What Differences do eBooks Have?

It's a hard one to get your head around, but eBooks do not have pages. Page numbers are irrelevant, and you strip all headers and footers out. Your book will look a little different on each device, re-sizing and flowing to fit the screen. Even the font size and line spacing can be set by the user, so there's no need to have different font sizes. You also do not set font colours.

Whereas with print books we can get all fancy, with eBook creation, we must make it plain. If you don't like this idea, just try to run a highly-formatted Word doc through an ePub wizard and wait for the migraine you'll get with all the error messages!

There are three types of eBooks: Fixed-layout, Reflowable, and Enhanced. You have a lot more to do to design multimedia files with video/audio and touch animations, so think carefully if you like de-signing first. The application *iBooks Author* lets you design an eBook with any type of element you want, as long as you don't mind that it's 'fixed' and only purchasable in iBookstore (Apple take 30%). Fixed-layout saves it similar to a print book, but it means the reader zooms in with their fingers and the text won't reflow: a bit of a burden.

The free Amazon program *Kindle Create* can be used to create a "reflowable" or Print Replica Kindle Package Format (KPF) file from a typeset PDF or from a stripped Word file. This solution could be ideal for non-fiction books with lots of images and tables, which cannot easily go through their usual 'automated' wizard. Either way, you'll need to be a quick learner or hire someone to help. Hiring someone is infinitely easier.

It's very important to take out lots of empty lines or tabs in your pre-eBook text.

Some Places to Sell your eBook

If you've got a countdown deal planned, try out some of these sites:

Instafreebie (free ebooks, engagement) **https://www.instafreebie.com/authors.** Free or US$20 p.m. to also collect emails of readers.

Free 99 Books (free & 0.99 ebooks) **http://www.free99books.com/**

Sellfy (ecommerce store to deliver your own ebooks) **https://sellfy.com** $29 p.m. + 2%

Reading Deals (33% off/free) **https://readingdeals.com/** Free (no guarantee) or US$29 - book must have 5 x 4-star+ reviews and proper formatting to be accepted for their huge reader base.

Ensure your advertising spend is commensurate with any financial benefit gained. Don't just pay $100 to advertise a free book if you have no other books listed.

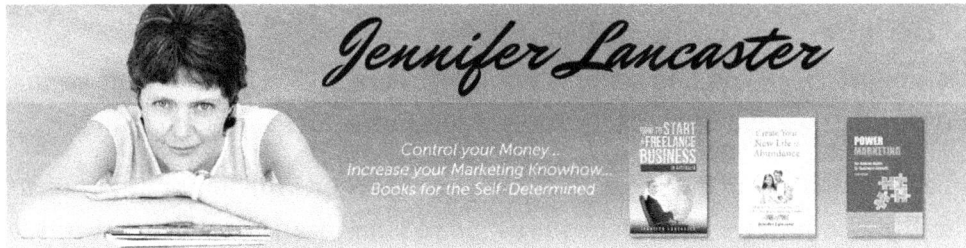

A Personal Brand Gives You the Edge

Do you realise the power of personal branding when it comes to marketing a book? The difference between you and a faceless corporation is "personality", "connectiveness", and "interaction". So use these things to give your overall profitability a leg up.

Personality: This incorporates your personal values, your ethics, your sunny smile, and your whole past experience. Embracing these in your branding and personal presentation builds rapport. Colours you wear can also feature in your website and book cover.

Connectiveness: Unlike big companies, you can answer the phone personally and reply to emails, texts, messages, blog comments. Meeting business folk at an event starts building a relationshp, one which you can continue. Connecting also includes helping them by recommending specialists whom you know (referrals).

Interaction: Social connectiveness is important to us all. The way that people tend to personally share or ask you questions these days is through social media. Make it easy for folks to connect with you this way by setting up:

- Facebook profile and business/fan page (linked to profile)
- LinkedIn (more important for B2B)
- Twitter

- Instagram
- GoToMeeting or Zoom
- Webinars, answering their questions at end (e.g. Zoom, Everwebinar)
- Video course with interactive questions for students and readers (e.g. Teachable, Thinkific).

Getting Book Reviews

You can request a book review for Amazon in a few select sites. This is not the same as an editorial review, which is what Kirkus and Blue Ink sell to help the author and aid their credibility.

Go to https://readersfavorite.com and post your Amazon ASIN or ISBN for your book, and it will find the details. The free reviews take 10-12 weeks, or you can pay US$59 and upward for much quicker reviews.

Reading Deals Review will place an order for 10-15 Amazon reviews + give the book 15 tweets, for US$79. **https://readingdeals.com/reviews**

Starting an Imprint?

Join the Australian Publishers Association (**https://www.publishers.asn.au/**) to help your micro publishing house along, with professional webinars, awards events, access to Frankfurt Book Fair for members, and access to TitlePage as a micro publisher.

Associate membership costs from $80 to $200, dependant on turnover.

A Media Tip

A well-placed article in an industry publication lets readers sample your book before they buy. Mention where they can find the book in your author byline or somewhere in the article itself. I wrote an article about freelancing in a local magazine and also scanned that article for use in my Instagram and Facebook accounts.

This all takes time, but with some regular effort, it will build a readership base. Although we can't all have newspaper columns or TV spots to aid our promotions, we can gradually inspire our tribe to look further into our best work. **Medium.com** is another place where anyone can gather readers for their theories, and talk about their upcoming book, without the hassle of owning a website.

What Types of Editing are Required?

Without a doubt, after initial idea and strategy, book editing is the most essential service for self-publishing authors. So what are the different types of editing, and what do you get?

Copy Editing.

A careful proofread, this includes for correcting errors in spelling, grammar, and punctuation. As well, the copy editor will check cross-references and standardise references. Some editing services also recommend a more thorough edit called a "Line Edit".

Line Editing.

This presumes the author has gone over their text to reduce errors and improve construction. This level is appropriate for those with complex prose or perhaps non-native speakers. If you read your paragraph aloud and find yourself straining for breath, then this editing work will fix it!

Your editor will include better flow suggestions, if seeing minor structure problems, and the odd rearrangement of sentences. However, if your writing is full of "challenges to understanding", is completely out of order, or is not structured on a theme, see below.

Developmental/Comprehensive editing.

Analysing non-fiction titles, this editing looks at your target readership, purpose of the book, and possible uses of the final book. Here, the editor examines whether the content is complete and appropriate, if the concepts are well developed, references complete and standardised, and ensures that material is well organised.

Comprehensive Editing inclusions:
- Correction of spelling and grammar (in the second round usually)
- Ensure consistency of voice/appropriate tone
- Check that illustrations, tables and bullet lists are used effectively throughout
- The initial review (suggestions to improve your book) may well save you a further round of editing
- Instructions for re-writing certain parts to improve the clarity, structure and flow
- Suggestions on removal of extraneous text (after review) or
- Suggestions on creating a more persuasive argument, e.g. with examples, evidence, and comparisons

- Your feedback and discussion of changes to keep.

Developmental reviews are usually given in a separate document. These involve suggestions on content, tone and audience fit. They will be cheaper than a full developmental edit.

Indexing is a separate service for topical non-fiction books and takes a fair amount of experience. The service price ranges from $2 to $4 per indexable page for a professional Index.

Book Typesetting (or Design) is also a not-so-simple endeavour if it's a non-fiction book with images, tables, or special boxes. You could budget anywhere from $400 to $1300 or more for this service.

Cover Design is another case of *you get what you pay for*. While some entrust their work to a design competition like 99Designs, which does *not* cost $99, I prefer recommending my usual designers, with their quotes of approx. $200 to $330 per paperback cover (with 3D or front cover jpeg as a bonus). Usually your typesetter will also offer to design the cover, so check out their online portfolio.

EBook covers are much easier and cheaper to produce, but you cannot take an eBook cover (e.g. from Fiverr) and magically turn it into a full-wrap cover, ready for the printer. Resolution does not go 'up'; it only works resizing downwards. So, if you've already had a nice eBook cover designed at 72 DPI, then ask that designer for a quote to make you a CMYK, 300 DPI full-wrap cover on the template from your printing house. You will need to decide on the back cover blurb. (DPI = dots per inch).

Also request the 'source' file, e.g. InDesign or Photoshop, so you can take that design and later make a new version or new book in the series. This is important for maintaining a consistent look throughout a series and is something I regret not doing.

Other Co-writing Options

If you want your message and story to be published but your writing is not at the level needed to engage, then consider writing coaching or co-authoring. Co-authoring is not as expensive as ghost writing, if you work with someone who is efficient at writing practices. You can also choose to write a chapter in someone else's book on a set theme.

Niche Book Marketing

If you have written a book, one of the best ways to make its glory known is through places where target readers are. From the offline: targeted advertisements, book club promotions, award submissions, content syndication; to the online: blogger outreach, targeted banner advertising, social media strategy, author marketing on FaceBook. These tactics can set your book apart from the slush-pile.

Australia: 22,832 titles published in 2017 (up from 8,600 in 2004)[1]. 55 million books sold. United States: 304,912 new titles and editions published in 2013[2].

It is a truth universally acknowledged that publishers are the main beneficiaries from writing, and receive the greatest financial benefits from an author's work.
- Jeremy Fisher (in paper for the ASA).

That's you, if you self-publish!

If you direct your publishing strategy towards a particular market, and don't rely on Amazon or your Print partner to do the work, self-publishing a niche book is extremely rewarding. If you find creative ways to reach your market through further writing and/or live trainings, you'll do pretty well.

Most readers understand and respect that writing a well-formed book takes both time and detailed knowledge. If the problem or desire that your 'tribe' has is important to them, then you simply need to find ways to shout out the primary benefits of the book's content in all your promotional efforts.

---

1   Source: BooksandPublishing.com

2   Source: Wikipedia.com

Resources for Marketing

The Government has made a Digital Business portal which explains about getting online, planning promotional activities, and creating/planning a website. This information can help you decide whether to make a website yourself or hire an outsourcer, and what website options exist. **Business.gov.au (http://www.digitalbusiness.gov.au/)**

BEC Australia (https://becaustralia.org.au/) — mentoring, analysis, business info, live training, grant information, networking with other businesses, Government links.

Australian Book Prizes
- The Stella Prize (for women authors of fiction or non-fiction)
- QWC/Hachette Australia Manuscript Development Program (Emerging Australian authors of commercial fiction/non-fiction over 55,000 wds).

Join the **Australian Society for Authors/ASA (https://www.asauthors.org/membership/)** for access to Book fairs, Legal contract services, Literary speed dating, and a Distribution Agreement with John Reed Books. Associate members: $11 p.m. Full membership, for published authors: $17 p.m. or $203 annually.

How to Get More Publishing Information?

Articles, videos, and training for non-fiction authors: **www.businessauthoracademy.com** (See the *Book Creation Success* page for our member offer)

More info on self-publishing or editing: **www.jenniferlancaster.com.au/blog**

IngramSpark Resources: **https://www.ingramspark.com/resources**

Other Books by Jennifer Lancaster:

How to Control your Financial Destiny

Create your New Life of Abundance

How to Start a Freelance Business in Australia

Power Marketing: An Aussie Guide to Business Growth

Available in the bookstore at: **www.JenniferLancaster.com.au/Books**